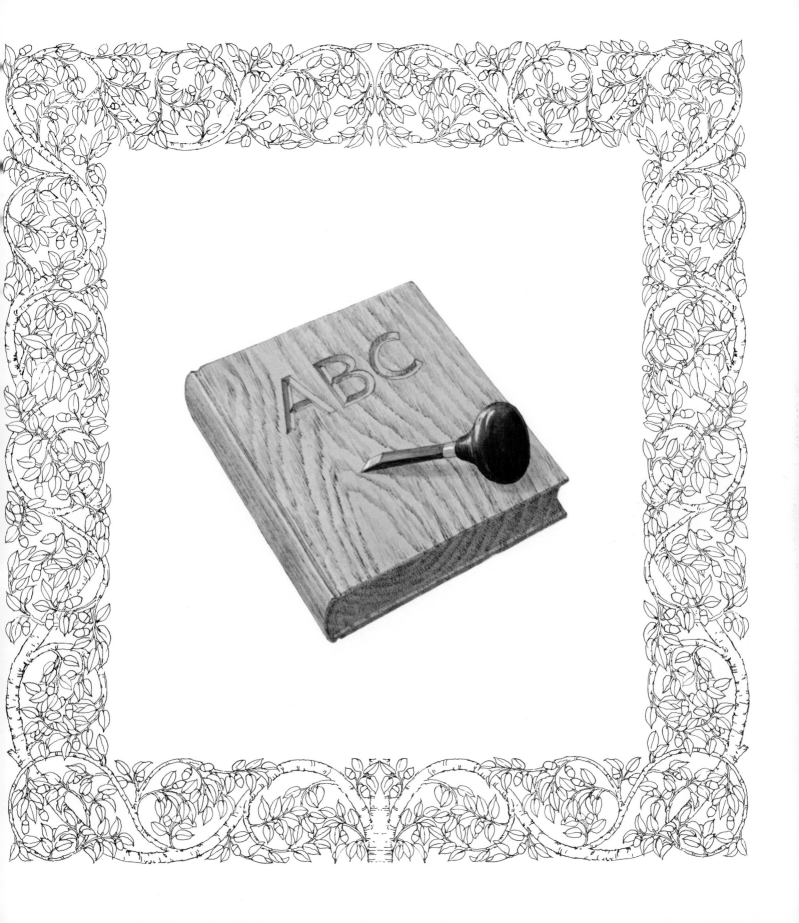

First United States Publication 1975. Printed in United States Copyright©1974 by Fukuinkan - Shoten.

Library of Congress Cataloging in Publication Data. Anno, Mitsumasa, 1926-, Anno's alphabet. SUMMARY: Each letter of the alphabet accompanies a full - page picture of an object whose name begins with that letter :   an-vil, bicycle, etc. [1. Alphabet books] I. Title. II.   Title : Alphabet. PZ 7. A 5875 An 3   [E]   73-21652 ISBN   0-690-00540-7   ISBN   0-690-00541-5   (lib. bdg.)

ANNO'S ALPHABET

— An Adventure in Imagination —

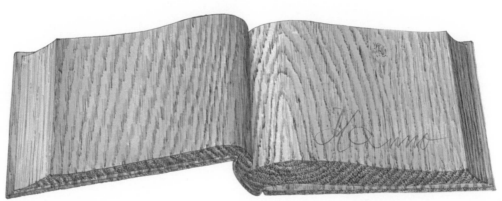

THOMAS Y. CROWELL COMPANY

NEW YORK

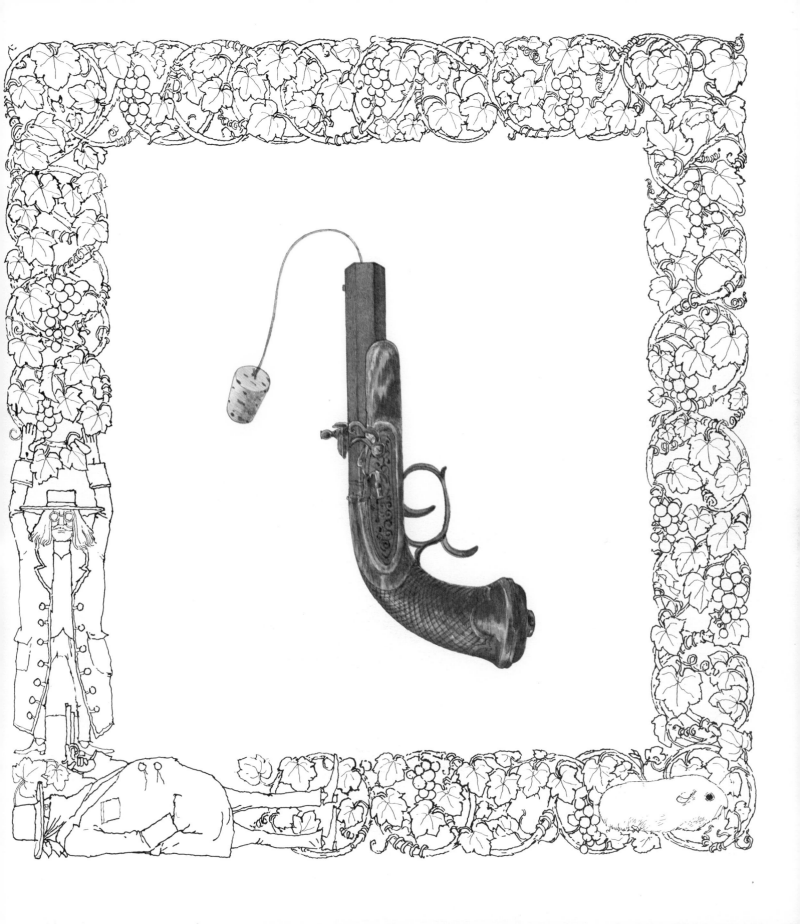

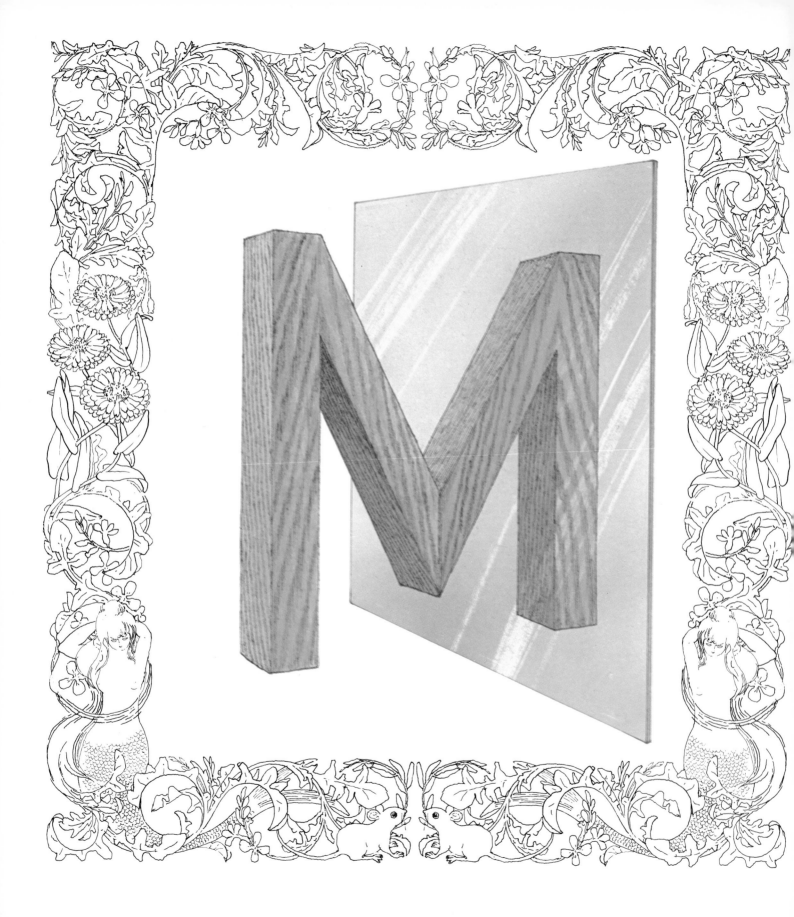

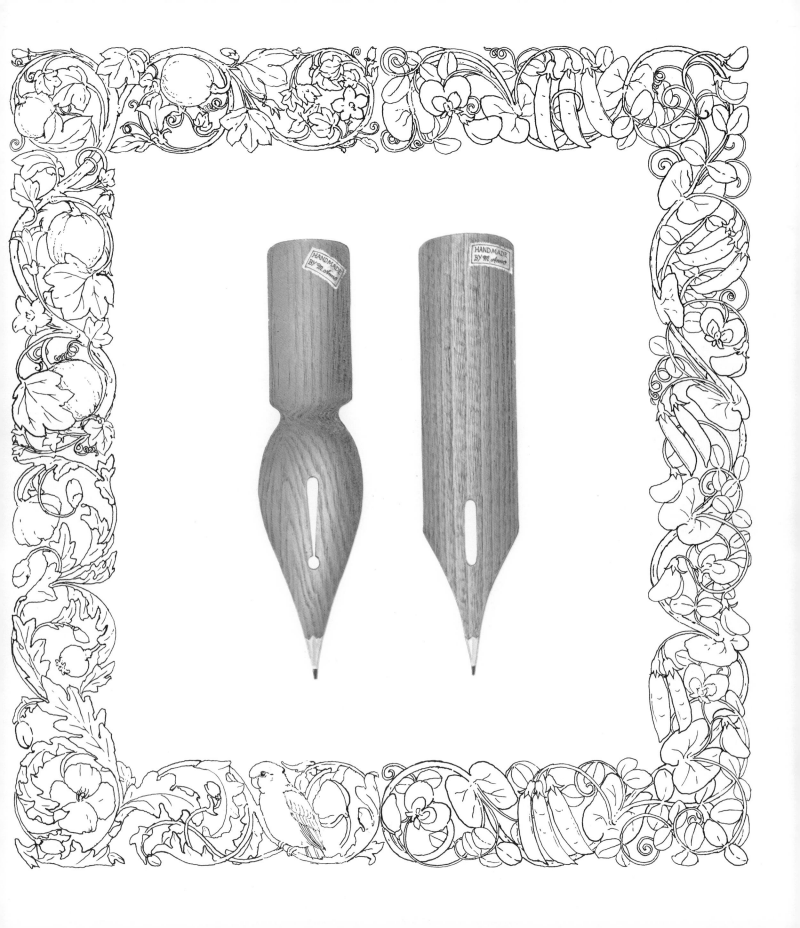

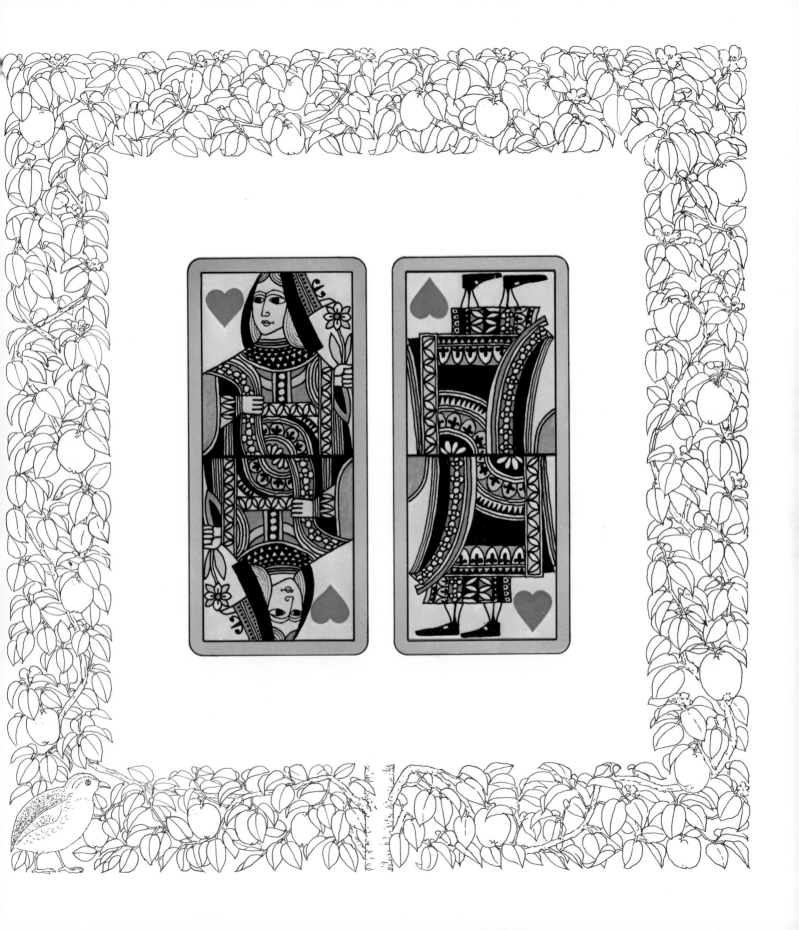

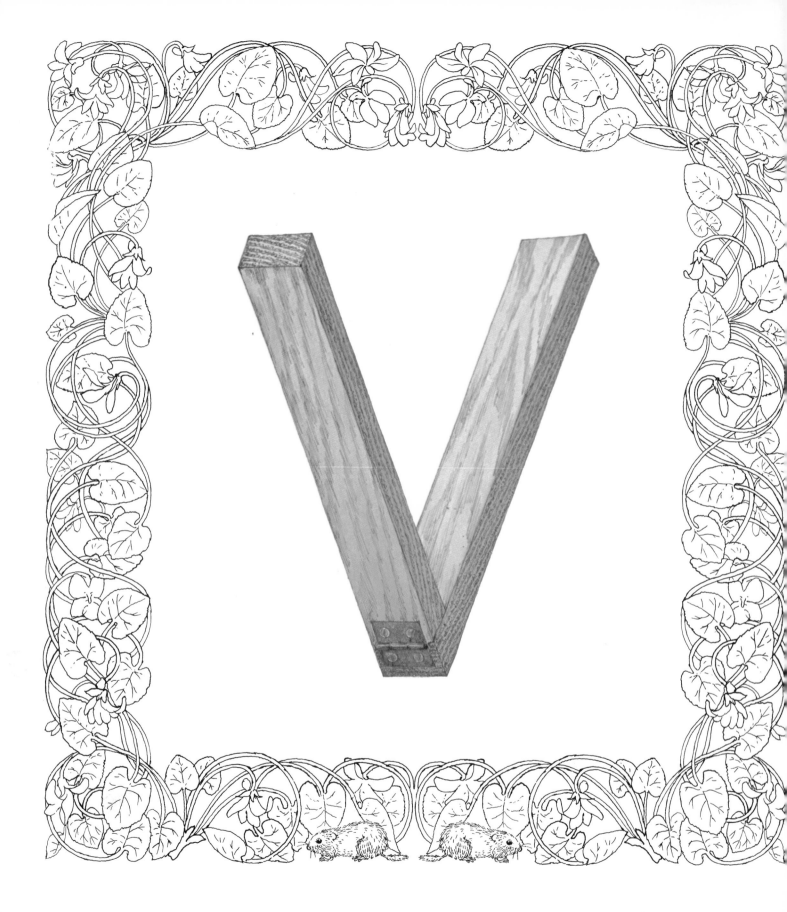

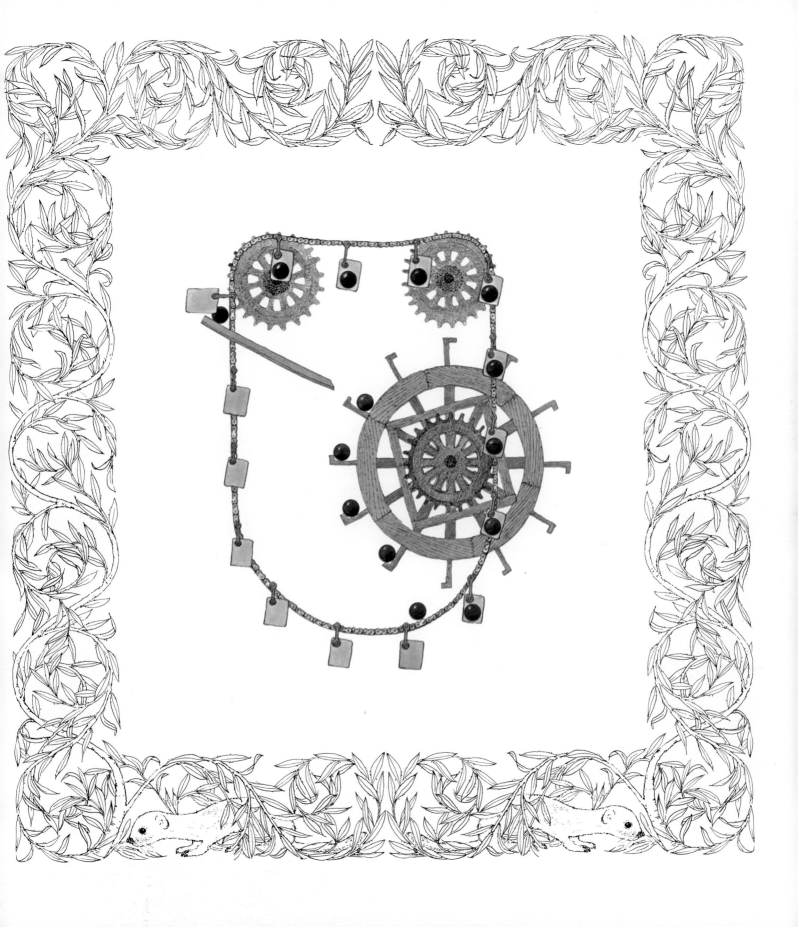

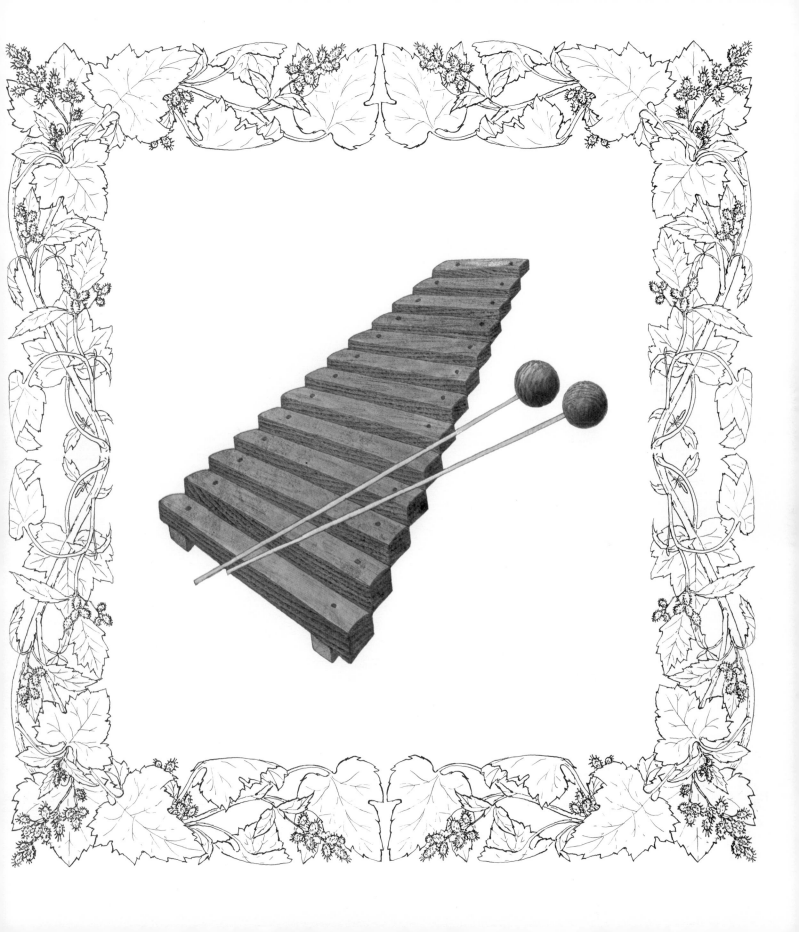

A guide to <u>some</u> of the things to be found in the pages of
Mr Anno's Alphabet.

A Anvil   Acanthus, anemone, ant, aster
B Bicycle   Bean, bee, bell, bird, button
C Clown in a Clock   Canary, child, clover
D Devil in a Die   Daisy, dove, duck, dwarf
E Eight Easter Eggs   Elf, *eschscholzia* (california poppy)
F Firemen with Fire-engine number Five   Fairy, forget-me-not
G Golden Gun   Gangster, gentleman, glasses, gloves, grapes,
                                           guinea-pig, gun

H Horn   Honeybee, hook, hops
I Ink   Iguana, impala, ivy
J Jester Juggling with Jacks   Jack, jasmine, jay
K Kangaroo with a Kerchief   Key, king, knapweed (cornflower), knife, knot
L Lock   Ladybird/ladybug, leopard, lily
M Map, Mirror   Marigold, mermaid, mouse, mustard
N Nut, Nut-cracker   Narcissus, nettle
O Orange Oil-paint   Olive, owl
P Pen and Pencil   Parrot, pea, poppy, pumpkin
Q Queen   Quail, quince
R Rocking-horse   Rabbit, rose
S Scales   Shepherd's purse, snake, spoon, stock
T Typewriter   Thistle, tiger
U Umbrella   Unicorn, *urena sinuata*
V Violin   Violet, vole
W Wheels   Weasel, willow
X Xylophone   *Xanthium strumarium* (burr-weed)
Y Yacht   Yarrow, yellow jacket (wasp), yew, yo-yo
Z Zebra   Zinnia

ABOUT THE AUTHOR

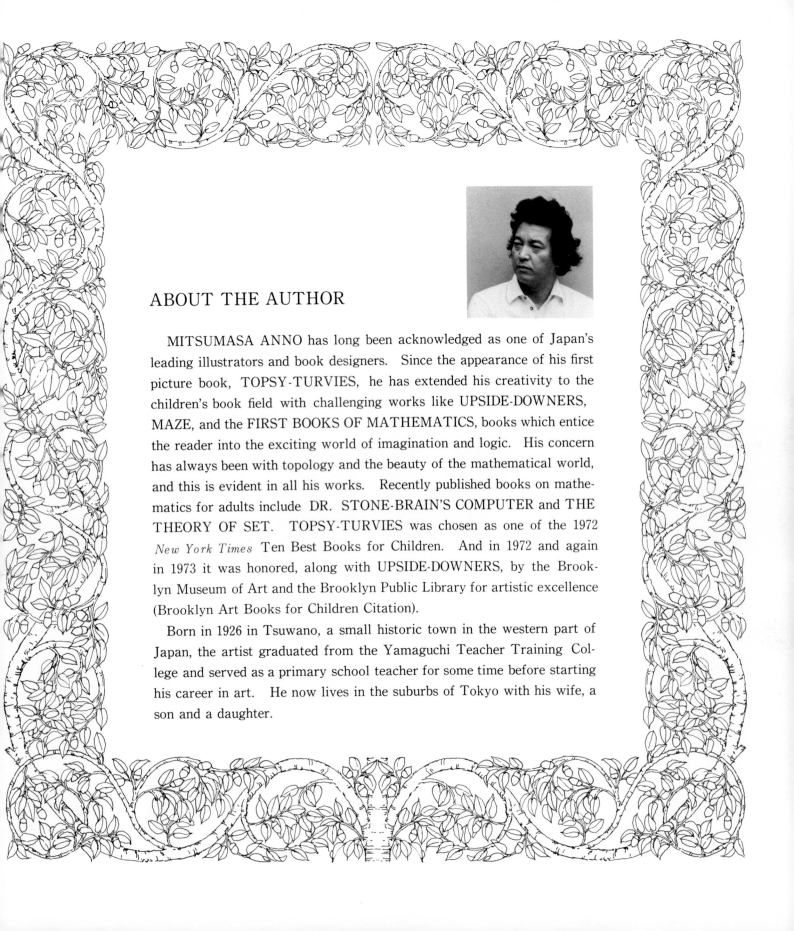

MITSUMASA ANNO has long been acknowledged as one of Japan's leading illustrators and book designers. Since the appearance of his first picture book, TOPSY-TURVIES, he has extended his creativity to the children's book field with challenging works like UPSIDE-DOWNERS, MAZE, and the FIRST BOOKS OF MATHEMATICS, books which entice the reader into the exciting world of imagination and logic. His concern has always been with topology and the beauty of the mathematical world, and this is evident in all his works. Recently published books on mathematics for adults include DR. STONE-BRAIN'S COMPUTER and THE THEORY OF SET. TOPSY-TURVIES was chosen as one of the 1972 *New York Times* Ten Best Books for Children. And in 1972 and again in 1973 it was honored, along with UPSIDE-DOWNERS, by the Brooklyn Museum of Art and the Brooklyn Public Library for artistic excellence (Brooklyn Art Books for Children Citation).

Born in 1926 in Tsuwano, a small historic town in the western part of Japan, the artist graduated from the Yamaguchi Teacher Training College and served as a primary school teacher for some time before starting his career in art. He now lives in the suburbs of Tokyo with his wife, a son and a daughter.